Learn to Read Biblical Hebrew ~ Volume 2

Learn to Read

Biblical Hebrew ~ Volume 2

~~~~~~~~~~~~~~~~~~~~~~~~~~~~~~~~~~~~

A Word for Word Examination of the Hebrew Words in the Ten Commandments

By Jeff A. Benner

Cover design by Jeff A. Benner.

"Learn to Read Biblical Hebrew, Volume 2," by Jeff A. Benner. ISBN 978-1-60264-905-7.

Published 2011 by Virtualbookworm.com Publishing Inc., P.O. Box 9949, College Station, TX 77845, US. ©2011, Jeff A. Benner. All rights reserved. Any part of this book may be copied for educational purposes only, without prior permission.

Manufactured in the United States of America.

Table of Contents

ACKNOWLEDGMENTS 1

INTRODUCTION 3

EXODUS 20:1 13

EXODUS 20:2 17

EXODUS 20:3 22

EXODUS 20:4 26

EXODUS 20:5 33

EXODUS 20:6 43

EXODUS 20:7 47

EXODUS 20:8 55

EXODUS 20:9 58

EXODUS 20:10 62

EXODUS 20:11 70

EXODUS 20:12 82

EXODUS 20:13 89

EXODUS 20:14 91

EXODUS 20:15 93

EXODUS 20:16 95

EXODUS 20:17 98

Acknowledgments

I would like to thank a group of people who have sacrificed of their time and talents to make corrections and suggestions for this book. Without them, this book would not be the quality that it is. My heartfelt thanks go out to each of these individuals.

Bryan Baker	Jerry Lambert
Bea Baldridge	Paul Lurk
Rob Black	Merlin
Ken Finn	Frances Stolz
Dee Kay	Ted Walther
Kay Kindall	Janet Wyckoff

Learn to Read Biblical Hebrew ~ Volume 2

Introduction

In my book *Learn to Read Biblical Hebrew* the reader learned the Hebrew alphabet and a few Hebrew words. In the final lesson the reader was introduced to basic Hebrew syntax, how sentences are constructed. This book is a continuation of that book and goes into greater detail about Hebrew verbs, nouns and adjectives, as well as their many prefixes and suffixes. First, in this introduction, we will examine how Hebrew verbs, nouns and adjectives are constructed. Then we will take a very close look at Exodus 20:1-17 (the Ten Commandments) and carefully examine every word in detail.

Transliteration of Hebrew into English

The following is a chart showing the English letters that are used to transliterate the Hebrew consonants and vowels.

Consonants					
א	Silent	ט	t	ף פ	ph
בּ	b	י	y	פ	p
ב	v	כ	k	צ ץ	ts
ג	g	כ ך	kh	ק	q
ד	d	ל	l	ר	r
ה	h	מ ם	m	שׁ	sh

ו v	נ ן n	שׁ s
ז z	ס s	ת t
ח hh	ע Silent	

Vowels

וֹ o	אֶ e	אֱ e
וּ u	אַ a	אֲ a
אֵ[1] e[2]	אָ a[3]	אָ a
אִ i	אֹ o	
אֵ ey	אֻ u	

Pronunciation of transliterated Hebrew words

Because Hebrew letters are pronounced a little differently than English, the following are the Hebrew pronunciation of the letters and letter combinations used in the transliteration of Hebrew words.

| a | like the "a" in father | m | like the "m" in me |
| ai | like the "ai" in aisle | n | like the "n" in no |

---

[1] The letter א (aleph) is not part of the vowel, but is used only to show the placement of the vowel pointing.

[2] In some cases this vowel is used as a syllable break, represented by an apostrophe, and is silent.

[3] On some rare occasions, this vowel pointing is pronounced "o."

b	like the "b" in boy	o	like the "o" in cold
d	like the "d" in dog	p	like the "p" in pie
e	like the "e" in egg	ph	like the "ph" in phone
ey	like the "ey" in grey	q	like the "k" in kite
g	like the "g" in go	r	like the "r" in road
h	like the "h" in hello	s	like the "s" in sit
hh	like the "ch" in the name Bach	sh	like the "sh" in shine
i	like the "i" in machine	t	like the "t" in tie
iy	like the "i" in machine	u	like the "u" in tune
k	like the "k" in kite	v	like the "v" in vine
kh	like the "ch" in the name Bach	y	like the "y" in yellow
l	like the "l" in lake	z	like the "z" in zebra

The Verb

A verb describes an action, such as the word "cut" in the sentence, "Jacob cut a tree." The one performing the action is called the subject. In this sentence, Jacob is the subject of the verb, the one doing the cutting. The one receiving the action of the verb is called the object. In this sentence, the tree is the object of the verb, the one being cut.

Verbs have a tense. In English, the three major tenses are past, present and future. The word "cut" is in the past tense while "cutting" is the present tense and "will cut" is the future tense.

In Hebrew, the verb, subject, and object work much the same way, but with some slight differences.

While English verb tenses are related to time, Hebrew verb tenses are related to action and there are only two: Perfect (a completed action) and imperfect (an incomplete action).

In English, the subject of the verb precedes the verb, but in Hebrew it follows the verb.

Most Hebrew verbs will identify the person (first, second or third), gender (masculine or feminine), and number (singular or plural) of the subject of the verb, and in some instances the person, gender, and number of the object.

Below are a few common verb conjugations of the Hebrew verb שמע (Sh-M-Ah[4], Strong's #8085). The bold letters are the prefixes and suffixes which identify the tense, person, and gender of the subject of the verb.

Perfect Tense

שָׁמַעְתִּי	shama**tiy**	**I** heard
שָׁמַעְתָּ	shama**ta**	**you** heard
שָׁמַע	shama	**he** heard
שָׁמְעָה	sham**ah**	**she** heard

---

[4] I should note that Hebrew verb stems, such as שמע, are not actual words and cannot be pronounced until they are conjugated. Therefore, I will simply transliterate each letter of the verb stems. For the verb stem שמע this will be "Sh" for the letter shin (ש), "M" for the letter mem (מ) and "Ah" for the letter ayin (ע).

Imperfect Tense		
אֶשְׁמַע	eshma	**I will** hear
תִּשְׁמַע	tishma	**you will** hear
יִשְׁמַע	yishma	**he will** hear
תִּשְׁמַע	tishma	**she will** hear

Below are a few common suffixes (in bold letters) that identify the object of a verb.

שְׁלָחַנִי	shelahha**niy**	he sent **me**
שְׁלָחֶךָ	shal'hhe**kha**	he sent **you**
שְׁלָחוֹ	shelahh**o**	he sent **him**

Besides the "simple" verbs (called qal verbs) used above, seven other verb forms are used that slightly change the meaning of the verb. However, we will only look at the three most common. The niphil is the passive form and adds the prefixed letter נ (ni). The hiphil is the causative form and adds the prefixed letter ה (hi) and the letter י (iy) as an infix.

7

The Hitpa'el is the reflexive form and adds the prefixed letters הת (hit).

Niphil	נִקְדַּשׁ	niq'dash	he **was** special
Hiphil	הִקְדִּישׁ	hiq'diysh	he **caused** to be special
Hitpa'el	הִתְקַדֵּשׁ	hit'qa'desh	he **made himself** special

A few other verb forms differ from those we have previously discussed. The first is the infinitive verb, which does not include a tense (perfect or imperfect), subject or object of the verb. It only identifies the action, such as "listen." The second is the imperative, which like the infinitive, does not include a tense or object, but it does identify the gender and number of the subject as well as the action of the verb, but more as a command, such as "listen!". The third is the participle, which is used much like our present tense verbs in English, such as "listening." Below are examples of these verb forms.

Infinitive	שָׁמֹעַ	shamo	listen
Imperative	שְׁמַע	shema	listen!
Participle	שֹׁמֵעַ	shomey	listening

The Noun

In our previous sentence, Jacob cut a tree, the words Jacob and tree are nouns. A noun is defined as a person, place or thing and some common examples of Hebrew nouns include; בן (*ben*-son), מלך (*melekh*-king), ארץ (*erets*-land), יד (*yad*-hand), חי (*hhai*-life) and עץ (*eyts*-tree). Proper nouns are names of specific persons and places such as יעקב (*Ya'aqov*-Jacob) and מצרים (*Mitsrayim*-Egypt).

Every Hebrew noun is either masculine or feminine. An obvious masculine noun is איש (*iysh*-man) and an obvious feminine noun would be אשה (*iyshah*-woman). As can be seen in this example, the suffix ה (*ah*) can be added to a masculine noun to make it feminine. Another example is the word מלך (*melek*-king), a masculine noun, whereas מלכה (*mal'khah*-queen) is the feminine form. However, some nouns cannot be identified as masculine or feminine by a suffix, or lack of it. The word עץ (*eyts*-tree) is masculine while רוח (*ru'ahh*-wind) is feminine. The gender of a noun is important, as will become evident in later lessons.

Masculine nouns are made plural by adding the ים (*iym*) suffix and feminine nouns are made plural by adding the ות (*ot*) suffix.

9

Articles, Conjunctions and Prepositions

Specific letters are used in Hebrew to represent the article, conjunction, and preposition and are prefixed to nouns (and sometimes verbs). Below are all of these prefixes (in bold) attached to the Hebrew noun אֶרֶץ (erets, Strong's #776).

Article	הָאָרֶץ	ha'arets	**the** land
Conjunction	וְאֶרֶץ	va'arets	**and** a land
Preposition	לְאֶרֶץ	la'arets	**to** a land
Preposition	בְּאֶרֶץ	be'erets	**in** a land
Preposition	מֵאֶרֶץ	me'erets	**from** a land
Preposition	כְּאֶרֶץ	ke'erets	**like** a land

Adjectives

An adjective is a word that provides description to a noun. For instance, the Hebrew word טוֹב (good) is a common adjective that can be found in the following phrase meaning "good day."

יוֹם טוֹב (yom tov)

Notice that in Hebrew the adjective follows the noun which it describes. If the noun is prefixed by the article הַ (ha), then the adjective will be as well, such as we see in the next phrase meaning "the good mountain."

הָהָר הַטּוֹב (hahar hatov)

The adjective will also match the gender of the noun. In the last two examples, the words יוֹם and הַר are masculine nouns therefore; the masculine form טוֹב is used. The word אֶרֶץ (land) is a feminine word so the feminine adjective טוֹבָה is used in the following phrase meaning "good land."

אֶרֶץ טוֹבָה (erets tovah)

The adjective will also match the number (singular or plural) of the noun. In each of our previous examples, the singular form of the word טוֹב is being used because the nouns it describes are singular. In the phrase, meaning "good houses," the word בֵּית (house) is written in the plural form, therefore the adjective is as well.

בָּתִּים טוֹבִים (batiym toviym)

11

Exodus 20:1

וַיְדַבֵּר אֱלֹהִים אֵת כָּל־הַדְּבָרִים הָאֵלֶּה לֵאמֹר:

וַיְדַבֵּר

Transliteration: vai-da-ber

Translation: and he spoke

Morphology: The root is the verb דבר (D-B-R, Strong's #1696) meaning "speak." The prefix י (ye) identifies the verb as imperfect tense—"will speak;" and the subject of the verb as third person masculine singular—"he will speak." The prefix ו (va) is a conjunction meaning "and," but also reverses the tense of the verb to the perfect tense—"and he spoke."

אֱלֹהִים

Transliteration: e-lo-hiym

Translation: powerful one

Morphology: The base word is the masculine noun אלוה (elo'ah, Strong's #433) meaning "power" or "powerful one." The יִם (iym) is the masculine plural suffix.

Comments: This plural noun is often used for someone or something of great importance or stature and the context of its use will determine if this word is being used as singular or plural.

Because this noun follows the verb, it is the subject of the verb, the "he" in "he spoke," and because the "he" is singular, this noun must be understood as a singular noun.

אֵת

Transliteration: eyt

Translation: [no translation for אֵת]

Morphology: The word אֵת (eyt, Strong's #853) is a particle that precedes the definite direct object of the previous verb.

כָּל

Transliteration: kol

Translation: all

Morphology: The word כל (kol, Strong's #3605) is a noun meaning "all."

הַדְּבָרִים

Transliteration: ha-de-va-riym

Translation: the words

Morphology: The base word is the masculine noun דבר (davar, Strong's #1697) meaning "word." The prefix ה (ha) is the article meaning "the." The suffix ים (iym) identifies this noun as plural.

הָאֵלֶּה

Transliteration: ha-ey-leh

Translation: the these

Morphology: The base word is the demonstrative pronoun אלה (ey-lah, Strong's #428) meaning "these." The prefix ה (ha) is the article meaning "the."

Comments: The words האלה and הדברים are combined to form a phrase meaning "these words." The phrase "all these words" is the definite direct object of the previous verb.

לֵאמֹר

Transliteration: ley-mor

Translation: to say / saying

Morphology: The root is the verb אמר (A-M-R, Strong's #559) meaning "say" and is written in the infinitive form.

The prefix ל (ley) is a preposition meaning "to"–"to say." This is best translated in context as "saying."

A Literal Translation

And the powerful one spoke all these words saying,

Exodus 20:2

אָנֹכִי יְהוָה אֱלֹהֶיךָ אֲשֶׁר הוֹצֵאתִיךָ
מֵאֶרֶץ מִצְרַיִם מִבֵּית עֲבָדִים:

אָנֹכִי

Transliteration: ah-no-khiy

Translation: I

Morphology: The word אנכי (anokhiy, Strong's #595) is the first person, singular pronoun—"I."

יְהוָה

Transliteration: YHVH

Translation: YHVH

Morphology: The word יהוה (YHVH, Strong's #3068) is a name derived from the verb הוה (H-Y-H, Strong's #1961) with the prefix י (y) identifying the subject of this verb as third person, masculine singular. Therefore this name means "he exists."

Comments: The vowel pointings attached to this word were never meant for the pronunciation of this name. Instead, they are the vowel pointings from the word אדוני (adonai, Strong's #136), which is the word Jews speak when they see the name יהוה. The original pronunciation of this name is uncertain.

אֱלֹהֶיךָ

Transliteration: eh-lo-hey-kha

Translation: your powerful one

Morphology: The base word is the noun אלוה (elo'ah, Strong's #433) meaning "power" or "powerful one." The ים (iym) is the masculine plural suffix, but in the construct state the letter ם (m) is dropped. The suffix ך (kha) is the second person, masculine singular, possessive pronoun—"of you" or "your."

Comments: This plural noun is often used for someone or something of great importance or stature and the context of its use will determine if this word is being used as singular or plural.

Because this noun is associated with the singular pronoun "I," this noun must be understood as a singular noun.

אֲשֶׁר

Transliteration: ah-sher

Translation: who

Morphology: The word אשר (asher, Strong's #834) is the relative participle that can mean "which," "that," "what" or "who."

הוֹצֵאתִיךָ

Transliteration: ho-tsey-tiy-kha

Translation: I made you go out

Morphology: The root is the verb יצא (Y-Ts-A, Strong's #3318) meaning "go out." The ה (h) prefix identifies this verb as a hiphil verb–"make go out." The suffix תי (ti) identifies the subject of the verb as first person, singular, and the tense of the verb as imperfect tense–"I will make go out". The suffix ךָ (kha) identifies the object of the verb as second person, masculine singular–"I will make you go out."

Comments: When the root word begins with the letter י (yud) and is preceded by another letter, in this case the letter ה (hey), the י (yud) is changed to a ו (vav).

מֵאֶרֶץ

Transliteration: mey-eh-rets

Translation: from a land

Morphology: The base word is the masculine noun ארץ (erets, Strong's #776) meaning "land," or "region." The prefix מ (mey) is a preposition meaning "from."

מִצְרַיִם

Transliteration: mits-ra-yim

Translation: Mitsrayim

Morphology: The word מצרים (mitsrayim, Strong's #4714) is a name often translated as "Egypt." This name is derived from the noun מצר (matsar) meaning "strait," with the double plural ים (yim) suffix. Therefore this name means "two straits."

Comments: When two nouns are placed together, such as with מארץ and מצרים, they are in the construct state and the word "of" would be placed between them in English—"from the land of Mitsrayim."

מִבֵּית

Transliteration: mi-beyt

Translation: from a house

Morphology: The base word is the masculine noun בית (bayit, Strong's #1004) meaning "house." The prefix מ (mi) is a preposition meaning "from."

עֲבָדִים

Transliteration: ah-vah-diym

Translation: slaves

Morphology: The base word is the masculine noun עבד (eved, Strong's #5650) meaning "slave." The suffix ים (iym) identifies this noun as a plural.

Comments: When two nouns are placed together, such as with מבית and עבדים, they are in the construct state and the word "of" would be placed between them in English—"from the house of slaves."

The phrases "from the land of Mitsrayim" and "from the house of slaves" are parallels, a common form of Hebrew poetry.

A Literal Translation

I am YHVH your powerful one, I made you go out from the land of Mitsrayim, from the house of slaves.

Exodus 20:3

לֹא יִהְיֶה־לְךָ אֱלֹהִים אֲחֵרִים עַל־פָּנָיַ׃

לֹא

Transliteration: lo

Translation: not

Morphology: The word לֹא (lo, Strong's #3808) is the negative participle meaning "not" and negates the action of the next verb.

יִהְיֶה

Transliteration: yih-yeh

Translation: he exists

Morphology: The root is the verb היה (H-Y-H, Strong's #1961) meaning "exist." The prefix י (yi) identifies the tense of the verb as imperfect tense, and the subject of the verb as third person, masculine singular—"he will exist."

Comments: Because of the negative participle preceding this verb, the verb will be translated as "he will not exist."

לְךָ

Transliteration: le-kha

Translation: for you

Morphology: This word does not contain any base word, but includes the prefix ל (le), a preposition meaning "for," and the second person, masculine singular pronoun suffix ךָ (kha) meaning "you."

אֱלֹהִים

Transliteration: e-lo-hiym

Translation: powerful one

Morphology: The base word is the masculine noun אלוה (elo'ah, Strong's #433) meaning "power" or "powerful one." The יִם (iym) is the masculine plural suffix.

Comments: This plural noun is often used for someone or something of great importance or stature and the context of its use will determine if this word is being used as singular or plural.

Because this noun follows the verb, it is the subject of the verb, the "he" in "he exists," and because the "he" is singular, this noun must be understood as a singular noun.

אֲחֵרִים

Transliteration: a-hhey-riym

Translation: other

Morphology: The base word is the adjective אחר (ahher, Strong's #312) meaning "other" or "another." The י (iym) is the masculine plural suffix.

Comments: This is an adjective describing אלהים. The gender and number of any adjective must match the gender and number of the noun it describes; therefore this adjective is written in the plural form to match the plurality of אלהים.

The phrase אלהים אחרים is the object of the previous verb, which identified the object as a masculine singular. So while this phrase could be translated as "other powerful ones" or "another powerful one," the context demands the latter translation.

עַל

Transliteration: al

Translation: upon

Morphology: The word על (al, Strong's #5921) is a preposition meaning "upon."

פָּנַי

Transliteration: pa-nai

Translation: my face

Morphology: The base word is פנה (paneh, Strong's #6437) meaning "face," but is always written in the plural form (paniym, Strong's #6440) by adding the suffix ים (iym). The suffix י (y) is the first person, singular, possessive pronoun—"of me" or "my."

Comments: The phrase על פני can be translated as "in my face," or better, "in my presence."

The following is a breakdown of the components of this word in order to explain its complex formation: פנה (paneh—noun) + ים (iym—plural suffix) + י (iy—possessive pronoun). Because of the plural suffix, the letter ה (hey) is dropped: פנ (pan) + ים (iym) + י (iy). When a plural noun is written in the construct state, the letter ם (mem) is also dropped: פנ (pan) + י (iy) + י (iy). The two י's (yuds) are then combined together: פנ (pan) + י (ai).

A Literal Translation

Another powerful one will not exist for you in my presence.

Exodus 20:4

לֹא תַעֲשֶׂה־לְךָ פֶסֶל וְכָל־תְּמוּנָה אֲשֶׁר
בַּשָּׁמַיִם מִמַּעַל וַאֲשֶׁר בָּאָרֶץ מִתַּחַת
וַאֲשֶׁר בַּמַּיִם מִתַּחַת לָאָרֶץ׃

לֹא

Transliteration: lo

Translation: not

Morphology: The word לֹא (lo, Strong's #3808) is the negative participle meaning "not" and negates the action of the next verb.

תַעֲשֶׂה

Transliteration: ta-a-seh

Translation: you will make

Morphology: The root is the verb עשה (Ah-S-H, Strong's #6213) meaning "do." The prefix ת (ta) identifies the verb as imperfect tense—"will do;" and the subject of the verb as second person masculine singular—"you will do."

Comments: This verb is used in a wide variety of applications and in the context of this verse has the idea of "make."

Because of the negative participle preceding this verb, the verb will be translated as "you will not make."

לְךָ

Transliteration: le-kha

Translation: for you

Morphology: This word does not contain any base word, but includes the prefix לְ (le), a preposition meaning "for," and the second person, masculine singular pronoun suffix ךָ (kha) meaning "you."

פֶּסֶל

Transliteration: pe-sel

Translation: sculpture

Morphology: The word פסל (pesel, Strong's #6459) is a masculine noun meaning "sculpture."

וְכָל

Transliteration: ve-khol

Translation: or any

Morphology: The base word is the noun כל (kol, Strong's #3605) meaning "all" or "any." The prefix ו (ve) is a conjunction meaning "and," but in context this is better translated as "or" in this verse.

תְּמוּנָה

Transliteration: te-mu-nah

Translation: resemblance

Morphology: The word תמונה (temunah, Strong's #8544) is a feminine noun meaning "resemblance."

אֲשֶׁר

Transliteration: ah-sher

Translation: which

Morphology: The word אשר (asher, Strong's #834) is the relative participle that can mean "which," "that," "what" or "who."

בַּשָּׁמַיִם

Transliteration: ba-sha-ma-yim

Translation: in the sky

Morphology: The base word is the masculine noun שמים (shamayim, Strong's #8064) meaning "sky." The prefix ב (ba) is a preposition meaning "in."

מִמַּעַל

Transliteration: mi-ma-al

Translation: above

Morphology: The base word is the adverb מעל (ma'al, Strong's #4605) meaning "upward." The prefix מ (mi) is a preposition meaning "from."

Comments: This word and prefix combination means "above."

וַאֲשֶׁר

Transliteration: va-a-sher

Translation: or which

Morphology: The word אשר (asher, Strong's #834) is the relative participle that can mean "which," "that," "what" or "who." The prefix ו (ve) is a conjunction meaning "and," but in context is better translated as "or" in this verse.

בָּאָרֶץ

Transliteration: ba-a-rets

Translation: in the land

Morphology: The base word is the masculine noun ארץ (erets, Strong's #776) meaning "land." The prefix ב (ba) is a preposition meaning "in."

Comments: The words "sky" and "land" are frequently used together and are an idiom for "everywhere" or "everything."

מִתַּחַת

Transliteration: mi-ta-hhat

Translation: below

Morphology: The base word is the noun תחת (tahhat, Strong's #8478) meaning "under." The prefix מ (mi) is a preposition meaning "from."

Comments: This word and prefix combination means "below."

וַאֲשֶׁר

Transliteration: va-a-sher

Translation: or which

Morphology: The word אשר (asher, Strong's #834) is the relative participle that can mean "which," "that," "what" or "who." The prefix ו (ve) is a conjunction meaning "and," but in context is better translated as "or" in this verse.

בַּמַּיִם

Transliteration: ba-ma-yim

Translation: in the water

Morphology: The base word is the masculine noun מים (mayim, Strong's #4325) meaning "water." The prefix ב (ba) is a preposition meaning "in."

מִתַּחַת

Transliteration: mi-ta-hhat

Translation: below

Morphology: The base word is the noun תחת (tahhat, Strong's #8478) meaning "under." The prefix מ (mi) is a preposition meaning "from."

Comments: This word and prefix combination means "below."

לָאָרֶץ

Transliteration: la-a-rets

Translation: to the land

Morphology: The base word is the masculine noun ארץ (erets, Strong's #776) meaning "land." The prefix ל (la) is a preposition meaning "to."

A Literal Translation

You will not make for yourself a sculpture or any resemblance which is in the skies above or which is in the land below or which is in the water below the land.

Exodus 20:5

לֹא־תִשְׁתַּחְוֶה לָהֶם וְלֹא תָעָבְדֵם כִּי
אָנֹכִי יְהֹוָה אֱלֹהֶיךָ אֵל קַנָּא פֹּקֵד עֲוֹן
אָבֹת עַל־בָּנִים עַל־שִׁלֵּשִׁים וְעַל־רִבֵּעִים
לְשֹׂנְאָי:

לֹא

Transliteration: lo

Translation: not

Morphology: The word לֹא (lo, Strong's #3808) is the negative participle meaning "not" and negates the action of the next verb.

תִשְׁתַּחְוֶה

Transliteration: tish-tahh-veh

Translation: you will bow yourself down

Morphology: The root is the verb שחה (Sh-Hh-H, Strong's #7812) meaning "bow down." The prefix ת (ti) identifies the tense of the verb as imperfect tense, and the subject of the verb as second person, masculine singular–"you will bow down." This verb is written in the hitpa'el form–"you will bow yourself down."

Comments: The hitpa'el form of a verb is usually identified with the prefix הת (hit), but this word uses a unique spelling where the ה (h) is dropped and the ת (t) is placed after the letter ש (sh). The addition of the letter ו (ve) is also a unique spelling of this word.

Because of the negative participle preceding this verb, the verb will be translated as "you will not bow yourself down."

לָהֶם

Transliteration: la-hem

Translation: to them

Morphology: This word does not contain any base word, but includes the prefix ל (le), a preposition meaning "for," and the third person, masculine plural pronoun suffix הם (hem) meaning "them."

וְלֹא

Transliteration: ve-lo

Translation: and not

Morphology: The word לֹא (lo, Strong's #3808) is the negative participle meaning "not" and negates the action of the next verb. The prefix ו (ve) is a conjunction meaning "and."

תַּעָבְדֵם

Transliteration: ta-av-deym

Translation: you will serve them

Morphology: The root is the verb עבד (Ah-B-D, Strong's #5647) meaning "serve." The prefix ת (ta) identifies the tense of the verb as imperfect tense, and the subject of the verb as second person, masculine singular–"you will serve." The suffix ם (m) identifies the object of the verb as third person, masculine plural–"you will serve them."

Comments: Because of the negative participle preceding this verb, the verb will be translated as "you will not serve them."

כִּי

Transliteration: kiy

Translation: because

Morphology: The word כי (kiy, Strong's #3588) is a conjunction meaning "because."

אָנֹכִי

Transliteration: ah-no-khiy

Translation: I

Morphology: The word אנכי (anokhiy, Strong's #595) is the first person, singular pronoun—"I."

יְהוָה

Transliteration: YHVH

Translation: YHVH

Morphology: The word יהוה (YHVH, Strong's #3068) is a name derived from the verb הוה (H-Y-H, Strong's #1961) with the prefix י (y) identifying the subject of this verb as third person, masculine singular. Therefore this name means "he exists."

Comments: The vowel pointings attached to this word were never meant for the pronunciation of this name. Instead, they are the vowel pointings from the word אדוני (adonai, Strong's #136), which is the word Jews speak when they see the name יהוה. The original pronunciation of this name is uncertain.

אֱלֹהֶיךָ

Transliteration: eh-lo-hey-kha

Translation: your powerful one

Morphology: The base word is the noun אלוה (elo'ah, Strong's #433) meaning "power" or "powerful one." The ים (iym) is the masculine plural suffix, but in the construct state the letter ם (m) is dropped. The suffix ך

36

(kha) is the second person, masculine singular, possessive pronoun—"of you" or "your."

Comments: This plural noun is often used for someone or something of great importance or stature and the context of its use will determine if this word is being used as singular or plural.

Because this noun is associated with the singular pronoun "I," this noun must be understood as a singular noun.

אֵל

Transliteration: eyl

Translation: mighty one

Morphology: The word אל (eyl, Strong's #410) is a masculine noun meaning "mighty one."

Comments: This noun is the root of אלוה (elo'ah, Strong's #433) and its plural form אלהים (elohiym, Strong's #430).

קַנָּא

Transliteration: qana

Translation: zealous

Morphology: The word קנא (qana, Strong's #7067) is an adjective meaning "zealous."

Comments: This adjective can also mean "jealous" or "envious" and is describing the previous noun אל.

פָּקֵד

Transliteration: po-qeyd

Translation: visiting

Morphology: The word פקד (P-Q-D, Strong's #6485) is a verb meaning "visit" and is written in the participle form (identified by the "o" and "ey" vowel pointings)– "visiting."

עָוֹן

Transliteration: ah-von

Translation: Twistedness

Morphology: The word עון (avon, Strong's #5771) is a masculine noun meaning "twisted one."

Comments: Hebrew nouns are frequently used as adjectives and can best be translated into English by adding the suffix "ness."

אָבֹת

Transliteration: ah-vot

Translation: fathers

Morphology: The base word is the masculine noun אב (av, Strong's #1) meaning "father." The suffix ת (ot) identifies this noun as plural.

Comments: Normally, the masculine plural suffix is written as ים (iym) and the feminine plural suffix as ות or

תֹ (ot). However, some masculine nouns use the וֹת or תֹ (ot) suffix.

When two nouns are placed together, such as with עָוֹן and אבת, they are in the construct state and the word "of" would be placed between them in the English— "twistedness of the fathers."

עַל

Transliteration: al

Translation: upon

Morphology: The word עַל (al, Strong's #5921) is a preposition meaning "upon."

בָּנִים

Transliteration: bah-niym

Translation: sons

Morphology: The base word is the masculine noun בֵּן (ben, Strong's #1121). The suffix ים (iym) identifies this noun as plural.

עַל

Transliteration: al

Translation: upon

Morphology: The word עַל (al, Strong's #5921) is a preposition meaning "upon."

שִׁלֵּשִׁים

Transliteration: shi-ley-shiym

Translation: third generations

Morphology: The base word is the masculine noun שלש (shileysh, Strong's #8029) meaning "third generation." The suffix יִם (iym) identifies this noun as plural.

וְעַל

Transliteration: ve-al

Translation: and upon

Morphology: The base word is the preposition עַל (al, Strong's #5921) meaning "upon." The prefix וַ (ve) is a conjunction meaning "and."

רִבֵּעִים

Transliteration: riy-bey-iym

Translation: fourth generations

Morphology: The base word is the masculine noun רבע (ribey, Strong's #7256) meaning "fourth generation." The suffix יִם (iym) identifies this noun as plural.

לְשֹׂנְאָי

Transliteration: le-son-ai

Translation: for the ones hating me

Morphology: The root is the verb שׂנא (saney, Strong's #8130) meaning "hate." This verb is written in the participle form (identified by the "o" and "e" vowel pointings)–"hating." The prefix ל (le) is a preposition meaning "for." The suffix יﬦ (iym) identifies the subject of the verb as plural–"for the ones hating." The suffix י (y) is the first person, singular pronoun–"for the ones hating me."

Comments: The following is a breakdown of the components of this word in order to explain its complex formation: ל (le–prefixed preposition) + שׂנא (soneh–participle verb) + יﬦ (iym–plural suffix) + י (iy–first person pronoun suffix). Because this verb is written in the construct state, the letter ﬦ (mem) is dropped: ל (le) + שׂנא (soneh) + י (iy) + י (iy). The two יs (yuds) are then combined together: ל (le) + שׂנא (soneh) + י (ai).

A Literal Translation

You will not bow yourself down to them, and you will not serve them, because I am YHVH your powerful one, a zealous mighty one, visiting the twistedness of the fathers upon the sons, upon the third and upon the fourth generations for the ones hating me.

Exodus 20:6

וְעֹשֶׂה חֶסֶד לַאֲלָפִים לְאֹהֲבַי וּלְשֹׁמְרֵי
מִצְוֹתָי׃

וְעֹשֶׂה

Transliteration: ve-oh-seh

Translation: and showing

Morphology: The root is the verb עשה (Ah-S-H, Strong's #6213) meaning "do," but is written in the participle form (identified by the "o" and "ey" vowel pointings)– "doing." The prefix ו (ve) is a conjunction meaning "and."

Comments: This verb is used in a wide variety of applications and in the context of this verse has the idea of "showing."

חֶסֶד

Transliteration: hhe-sed

Translation: respect

Morphology: The word חסד (hhesed, Strong's #2617) is a noun literally meaning to bow the head as a sign of respect to another.

43

לַאֲלָפִים

Transliteration: la-a-la-phiym

Translation: to the thousands

Morphology: The base word is the masculine noun אלף (aleph, Strong's #505) meaning "thousand." The prefix ל (la) means "to the" and the suffix יִם (iym) makes the noun plural.

לְאֹהֲבַי

Transliteration: le-o-ha-vai

Translation: for the ones loving me

Morphology: The root is the verb אהב (A-H-B, Strong's #157) meaning "love." This verb is written in the participle form (identified by the "o" and "a" vowel pointings)–"loving." The prefix ל (le) is a preposition meaning "for." The suffix יִם (iym) identifies the subject of the verb as plural–"for the ones loving." The suffix י (y) is the first person, singular pronoun–"for the ones loving me."

Comments: The following is a breakdown of the components of this word in order to explain its complex formation: ל (le–prefixed preposition) + אהב (ohav–participle verb) + יִם (iym–plural suffix) + י (iy–first person pronoun suffix). Because this verb is written in the construct state, the letter ם (mem) is dropped: ל (le) + אהב (ohav) + י (iy) + י (iy). The two יs (yuds) are then combined together: ל (le) + אהב (ohav) + י (ai).

וּלְשֹׁמְרֵי

Transliteration: ul-shom-rey

Translation: and for the guarding of

Morphology: The root is the verb שמר (Sh-M-R, Strong's #8104) meaning "guard." This verb is written in the participle form (identified by the "o" and "e" vowel pointings)–"guarding." The prefix ו (u) is the conjunction meaning "and." The prefix ל (le) is a preposition meaning "for." The suffix ים (iym) identifies the subject of the verb as plural, but when in the construct state, the letter מ (mem) is dropped–"and for the guarding of."

מִצְוֹתָי

Transliteration: mits-vo-tai

Translation: my directions

Morphology: The base word is the feminine noun מצוה (mitsvah, Strong's #4687) meaning "direction." The suffix ת (ot) identifies this noun as plural–"directions." The suffix י (y) is the first person, singular, possessive pronoun–"of me" or "my."

Comments: The following is a breakdown of the components of this word in order to explain its complex formation: מצוה (mitzvah–noun) + ות (ot–plural suffix) + י (iy–possessive pronoun). When a feminine noun ending with the letter ה (hey) adds the plural suffix ות, the ה is dropped from the word–מצו (mitsv) + ות (ot) + י (iy). The feminine plural suffix ות (ot) is often shortened to ת (ot)

45

מצו– (mitsv) + ת (ot) + י (iy). When a feminine plural noun is written in the construct state, the possessive pronoun י (iy) becomes י (ai) –מצו (mitsv) + ת (ot) + י (ai).

A Literal Translation

And showing respect to thousands for the ones loving me and for the guarding of my directions.

Exodus 20:7

לֹא תִשָּׂא אֶת־שֵׁם־יְהוָה אֱלֹהֶיךָ לַשָּׁוְא
כִּי לֹא יְנַקֶּה יְהוָה אֵת אֲשֶׁר־יִשָּׂא
אֶת־שְׁמוֹ לַשָּׁוְא׃

לֹא

Transliteration: lo

Translation: not

Morphology: The word לֹא (lo, Strong's #3808) is the negative participle meaning "not" and negates the action of the next verb.

תִשָּׂא

Transliteration: ti-sa

Translation: you will lift up

Morphology: The root is the verb נשא (N-S-A, Strong's #5375) meaning "lift up." The prefix ת (ti) identifies the tense of the verb as imperfect tense, and the subject of the verb as second person, masculine singular - you will lift up.

Comments: When a verb beginning with the letter נ (n) is conjugated, the נ (n) drops off.

This verb is used in a wide variety of applications and in the context of this verse has the idea of "representing."Because of the negative participle preceding this verb, the verb will be translated as "you will not lift up."

אֵת

Transliteration: et

Translation: [no translation for אֵת]

Morphology: The word אֵת (eyt, Strong's #853) is a particle that precedes the definite direct object of the previous verb.

שֵׁם

Transliteration: sheym

Translation: name

Morphology: The word שֵׁם (sheym, Strong's #8034) is a masculine noun meaning "name," but a more Hebraic meaning is "character."

יְהוָה

Transliteration: YHVH

Translation: YHVH

Morphology: The word יהוה (YHVH, Strong's #3068) is a name derived from the verb הוה (H-Y-H, Strong's #1961) with the prefix י (y) identifying the subject of this verb as third person, masculine singular. Therefore this name means "he exists."

Comments: The vowel pointings attached to this word were never meant for the pronunciation of this name. Instead, they are the vowel pointings from the word אדוני (adonai, Strong's #136), which is the word Jews speak when they see the name יהוה. The original pronunciation of this name is uncertain.

אֱלֹהֶיךָ

Transliteration: eh-lo-hey-kha

Translation: your powerful one

Morphology: The base word is the noun אלוה (elo'ah, Strong's #433) meaning "power" or "powerful one." The ים (iym) is the masculine plural suffix, but in the construct state the letter ם (m) is dropped. The suffix ך (kha) is the second person, masculine singular, possessive pronoun—"of you" or "your."

Comments: This plural noun is often used for someone or something of great importance or stature and the context of its use will determine if this word is being used as singular or plural.

Because this word is describing YHVH, a singular, this noun is being used as a singular. The phrase "name of

YHVH your powerful one" is the definite direct object of the preceding verb.

לַשָּׁוְא

Transliteration: la-sha-ve

Translation: as false

Morphology: The base word is the masculine noun שׁוא (shaveh, Strong's #7723) meaning "false." The prefix לְ (la) is a preposition meaning "to," but can also be translated as "as."

כִּי

Transliteration: kiy

Translation: because

Morphology: The word כִּי (kiy, Strong's #3588) is a conjunction meaning "because."

לֹא

Transliteration: lo

Translation: not

Morphology: The word לֹא (lo, Strong's #3808) is the negative participle meaning "not" and negates the action of the next verb.

יְנַקֶּה

Transliteration: ye-na-qeh

Translation: he will acquit

Morphology: The root is the verb נקה (N-Q-H, Strong's #5352) meaning "acquit." The prefix י (ye) identifies the verb as imperfect tense, and the subject of the verb as third person, masculine singular—"he will acquit."

Comments: Because of the negative participle preceding this verb, the verb is translated as "he will not acquit."

יְהוָה

Transliteration: YHVH

Translation: YHVH

Morphology: The word יהוה (YHVH, Strong's #3068) is a name derived from the verb הוה (H-Y-H, Strong's #1961) with the prefix י (y) identifying the subject of this verb as third person, masculine singular. Therefore this name means "he exists."

Comments: The vowel pointings attached to this word were never meant for the pronunciation of this name. Instead, they are the vowel pointings from the word אדוני (adonai, Strong's #136), which is the word Jews speak when they see the name יהוה. The original pronunciation of this name is uncertain.

אֵת

Transliteration: eyt

Translation: [no translation for אֵת]

Morphology: The word אֵת (eyt, Strong's #853) is a particle that precedes the definite direct object of the previous verb.

אֲשֶׁר

Transliteration: ah-sher

Translation: who

Morphology: The word אשר (asher, Strong's #834) is the relative participle that can mean "which," "that," "what" or "who."

יִשָּׂא

Transliteration: yi-sa

Translation: he will lift up

Morphology: The root is the verb נשא (N-S-A, Strong's #5375) meaning "lift up." The prefix י (yi) identifies the tense of the verb as imperfect tense, and the subject of the verb as third person, masculine singular - he will lift up.

Comments: When a verb beginning with the letter נ (n) is conjugated, the נ (n) drops off.

This verb is used in a wide variety of applications and in the context of this verse has the idea of "representing." The phrase "who lifts up" is the definite direct object of the preceding verb.

אֵת

Transliteration: et

Translation: [no translation for את]

Morphology: The word את (eyt, Strong's #853) is a particle that precedes the definite direct object of the previous verb.

שְׁמוֹ

Transliteration: sh-mo

Translation: his name

Morphology: The word שם (sheym, Strong's #8034) is a masculine noun meaning "name," but from a more Hebraic perspective means "character." The suffix ו (o) is the third person, masculine singular, and possessive pronoun–"of him or his."

Comments: This word is also a definite direct object of the preceding verb.

לַשָּׁוְא

Transliteration: la-sha-ve

Translation: as false

Morphology: The base word is the masculine noun שׁוא (shaveh, Strong's #7723) meaning "false." The prefix לְ (la) is a preposition meaning "to," but can also be translated as "as."

A Literal Translation

You will not lift up the name of YHVH your powerful one as false, because YHVH will not acquit one who lifts up his name as false.

Exodus 20:8

זָכוֹר אֶת־יוֹם הַשַּׁבָּת לְקַדְּשׁוֹ׃

זָכוֹר

Transliteration: za-khor

Translation: remember

Morphology: The word זכר (Z-K-R, Strong's #2142) is a verb, written in the infinitive form, meaning to "remember."

Comments: This verb does not have the meaning of remembering something that was forgotten, but instead to remember something in memorial or reflection. In this case it is remembering that YHVH ceased (but usually translated as rested) on the seventh day as we see in Genesis 2:2.

אֶת

Transliteration: et

Translation: [no translation for את]

Morphology: The word את (eyt, Strong's #853) is a particle that precedes the definite direct object of the previous verb.

יוֹם

Transliteration: yom

Translation: day

Morphology: The word יוֹם (yom, Strong's #3117) is a masculine noun meaning "day."

הַשַּׁבָּת

Transliteration: ha-shab-bat

Translation: the ceasing

Morphology: The base word is the noun שבת (Shabbat, Strong's #7676) meaning "ceasing." The prefix ה (ha) is the article meaning "the."

Comments: When two nouns are placed together, such as with יום and השבת, they are in the construct state and the word "of" would be placed between them in the English–"the day of ceasing" (note that the article shifts to the first noun in the phrase).

This phrase is the definite direct object of the previous verb.

לְקַדְּשׁוֹ

Transliteration: le-qad-sho

Translation: to set him apart as special

Morphology: The root is the verb קדש (Q-D-Sh, Strong's #6942) meaning "set apart for a special purpose" and is written in the infinitive form. The prefix ל (le) is a preposition meaning "for." The suffix ו (o) identifies the object of the verb as third person, masculine singular– "him."

Comments: The "him" is referring to the "day," a masculine word in Hebrew.

A Literal Translation

Remember the day of ceasing to set him apart as special.

Exodus 20:9

שֵׁשֶׁת יָמִים תַּעֲבֹד וְעָשִׂיתָ כָּל־מְלַאכְתֶּךָ :

שֵׁשֶׁת

Transliteration: shey-shet

Translation: six

Morphology: The word ששה (shishah, Strong's #8337) is an adjective meaning "six."

Comments: Because this word ends with the letter ה (hey), and is in construct state, the ה is converted to a ת (tav).

This word is normally used as an adjective, but in Hebrew, nouns and adjectives are interchangeable. This word must be understood as a noun and not an adjective for three reasons. First, as mentioned above, this word is in the construct state, which cannot occur with an adjective. Secondly, Hebrew adjectives always follow the noun it is describing. Since this word precedes the following noun it cannot be an adjective. Thirdly, Hebrew adjectives match the plurality or singularity of the noun it is describing. The following noun is plural and this word is singular. If this word was an adjective, it would also be in the plural.

יָמִים

Transliteration: yah-mim

Translation: days

Morphology: The base word is the masculine noun יום (yom, Strong's #3117) meaning "day." The suffix ים (iym) identifies the noun as plural.

Comments: When two nouns are placed together, such as with ששת and ימים, they are in the construct state and the word "of" would be placed between them in English—"six of the days."

תַעֲבֹד

Transliteration: tah-ah-vod

Translation: you will serve

Morphology: The root is the verb עבד (Ah-B-D, Strong's #5647) meaning "serve." The prefix ת (ta) identifies the verb as imperfect tense—"will serve;" and the subject of the verb as second person masculine singular—"you will serve."

וְעָשִׂיתָ

Transliteration: ve-ah-siy-tah

Translation: and you will do

Morphology: The root is the verb עשה (Ah-S-H, Strong's #6213) meaning "do." The suffix ת (ta) identifies the verb as perfect tense—"did;" and the subject of the verb as second person masculine singular—"you did." The prefix ו (ve) is the conjunction meaning "and," but also reverses the tense of the verb to imperfect tense—"you will do."

כָּל

Transliteration: kol

Translation: all

Morphology: The word כל (kol, Strong's #3605) is a noun meaning "all."

מְלַאכְתֶּךָ

Transliteration: me-lakh-teh-kha

Translation: your business

Morphology: The base word is the feminine noun מלאכה (melakhah, Strong's #4399) meaning "business." The suffix ך (kha) is the second person, masculine singular, possessive pronoun—"of you" or "your."

Comments: When a feminine noun ends with the letter ה (hey) and is in construct state, the ה is converted to a ת (tav).

A Literal Translation

Six of the days you will serve and you will do all your work.

Exodus 20:10

וְיוֹם הַשְּׁבִיעִי שַׁבָּת לַיהוָה אֱלֹהֶיךָ
לֹא־תַעֲשֶׂה כָל־מְלָאכָה אַתָּה
וּבִנְךָ־וּבִתֶּךָ עַבְדְּךָ וַאֲמָתְךָ וּבְהֶמְתֶּךָ
וְגֵרְךָ אֲשֶׁר בִּשְׁעָרֶיךָ׃

וְיוֹם

Transliteration: ve-yom

Translation: and day

Morphology: The base word is the masculine noun יוֹם (yom, Strong's #3117) meaning "day." The prefix וְ (ve) is a conjunction meaning "and."

הַשְּׁבִיעִי

Transliteration: hash-viy-iy

Translation: the seventh

Morphology: The base word is the adjective שְׁבִיעִי (sheviyiy, Strong's #7637) meaning "seventh." The prefix הַ (ha) is the article meaning "the."

Comments: This adjective is describing the previous word, so the phrase "and-day the-seventh" would be translated as "and the seventh day."

שַׁבָּת

Transliteration: shab-bat

Translation: ceasing

Morphology: The word שבת (Shabbat, Strong's #7676) is a noun meaning "ceasing."

Comments: This word is always used in the Hebrew Bible for the seventh day, the Shabbat (or Sabbath), the day work ceases for the purpose of rest.

לַיהוָה

Transliteration: la-YHVH

Translation: for YHVH

Morphology: The word יהוה (YHVH, Strong's #3068) is a name derived from the verb הוה (H-Y-H, Strong's #1961) with the prefix י (y) identifying the subject of this verb as third person, masculine singular. Therefore this name means "he exists." The prefix ל (la) is a preposition meaning "for."

Comments: The vowel pointings attached to this word were never meant for the pronunciation of this name. Instead, they are the vowel pointings from the word אדוני (adonai, Strong's #136), which is the word Jews speak when they see the name יהוה. The original pronunciation of this name is uncertain.

אֱלֹהֶיךָ

Transliteration: eh-lo-hey-kha

Translation: your powerful one

Morphology: The base word is the noun אלוה (elo'ah, Strong's #433) meaning "power" or "powerful one." The יֵם (iym) is the masculine plural suffix, but in the construct state the letter ם (m) is dropped. The suffix ך (kha) is the second person, masculine singular, possessive pronoun—"of you" or "your."

Comments: This plural noun is often used for someone or something of great importance or stature and the context of its use will determine if this word is being used as singular or plural.

Because this word is describing YHVH, a singular, this noun is being used as a singular.

לֹא

Transliteration: lo

Translation: not

Morphology: The word לֹא (lo, Strong's #3808) is the negative participle meaning "not" and negates the action of the next verb.

תַּעֲשֶׂה

Transliteration: ta-a-seh

Translation: you will do

Morphology: The root is the verb עשה (Ah-S-H, Strong's #6213) meaning "do." The prefix ת (ta) identifies the verb as imperfect tense—"will do;" and the subject of the verb as second person masculine singular—"you will do."

Comments: Because of the negative participle preceding this verb, the verb will be translated as "you will not do."

כָּל

Transliteration: khol

Translation: any

Morphology: The word כל (kol, Strong's #3605) is a noun meaning "all" or "any."

מְלָאכָה

Transliteration: me-la-khah

Translation: business

Morphology: The word מלאכה (melakhah, Strong's #4399) is a feminine noun meaning "business."

אַתָּה

Transliteration: a-tah

Translation: you

Morphology: The word אתה (atah, Strong's #859) is the second person, masculine singular pronoun—"you."

וּבִנְךָ

Transliteration: u-viyn-kha

Translation: or your son

Morphology: The base word is the masculine noun בן (ben, Strong's #1121) meaning "son." The prefix ו (u) is the conjunction meaning "and," but in context this is better translated as "or" in this verse. The suffix ךָ (kha) is the second person, masculine singular, possessive pronoun—"of you" or "your."

וּבִתֶּךָ

Transliteration: u-vi-teh-kha

Translation: or your daughter

Morphology: The base word is the feminine noun בת (bat, Strong's #1323) meaning "daughter." The prefix ו (u) is the conjunction meaning "and," but in context this is better translated as "or" in this verse. The suffix ךָ (kha) is the second person, masculine singular, possessive pronoun—"of you" or "your."

עַבְדְּךָ

Transliteration: av-deh-kha

Translation: your slave

Morphology: The base word is the masculine noun עבד (eved, Strong's #5650) meaning "slave." The suffix ךָ (kha) is the second person, masculine singular, possessive pronoun—"of you" or "your."

וַאֲמָתְךָ

Transliteration: va-a-mat-kha

Translation: or your maid-servant

Morphology: The base word is the feminine noun אמה (amah, Strong's #519) meaning "maid-servant." The prefix ו (va) is the conjunction meaning "and," but in context this is better translated as "or" in this verse. The suffix ךָ (kha) is the second person, masculine singular, possessive pronoun—"of you" or "your."

Comments: When a feminine noun ends with the letter ה (hey) and is in construct state, the ה is converted to a ת (tav).

וּבְהֶמְתֶּךָ

Transliteration: uv-hem-teh-kha

Translation: or your livestock

Morphology: The base word is the feminine noun בהמה (behemah, Strong's #929) meaning "livestock." The prefix ו (u) is the conjunction meaning "and," but in context this is better translated as "or" in this verse. The suffix ך (kha) is the second person, masculine singular, possessive pronoun—"of you" or "your."

Comments: When a feminine noun ends with the letter ה (hey) and is in construct state, the ה is converted to a ת (tav).

וְגֵרְךָ

Transliteration: ve-ger-kha

Translation: and your stranger

Morphology: The base word is the noun גר (ger, Strong's #1616) meaning "stranger," a foreigner who dwells and lives with the natives. The prefix ו (ve) is the conjunction meaning "and," but in context this is better translated as "or" in this verse. The suffix ך (kha) is the second person, masculine singular, possessive pronoun—"of you" or "your."

אֲשֶׁר

Transliteration: ah-sher

Translation: who

Morphology: The word אשר (asher, Strong's #834) is the relative participle that can mean "which," "that," "what" or "who."

בִּשְׁעָרֶיךָ

Transliteration: bish-a-rey-kha

Translation: in your gates

Morphology: The base word is the masculine noun שער (sha'ar, Strong's #8179) meaning "gate." The prefix בּ (ba) is a preposition meaning "in"–"in the gate." The suffix ים (iym) identifies this noun as plural, but in the construct state the letter ם (m) is dropped–"in the gates." The suffix ך (kha) is the second person, masculine singular, possessive pronoun–"in your gates."

A Literal Translation

And the seventh day is a ceasing for YHVH, your powerful one; you will not do any business, you or your son or your daughter, your slave or your maid-servant or your livestock or your stranger who is in your gates.

69

Exodus 20:11

כִּי שֵׁשֶׁת־יָמִים עָשָׂה יְהוָה
אֶת־הַשָּׁמַיִם וְאֶת־הָאָרֶץ אֶת־הַיָּם
וְאֶת־כָּל־אֲשֶׁר־בָּם וַיָּנַח בַּיּוֹם הַשְּׁבִיעִי
עַל־כֵּן בֵּרַךְ יְהוָה אֶת־יוֹם הַשַּׁבָּת
וַיְקַדְּשֵׁהוּ׃

כִּי

Transliteration: kiy

Translation: because

Morphology: The word כי (kiy, Strong's #3588) is a conjunction meaning "because."

שֵׁשֶׁת

Transliteration: shey-shet

Translation: six

Morphology: The word ששה (shishah, Strong's #8337) is an adjective meaning "six."

Comments: Because this word ends with the letter ה (hey), and is in construct state, the ה is converted to a ת (tav).

This word is normally used as an adjective, but in Hebrew, nouns and adjectives are interchangeable. This word must be understood as a noun and not an adjective for three reasons. First, as mentioned above, this word is in the construct state, which cannot occur with an adjective. Secondly, Hebrew adjectives always follow the noun it is describing. Since this word precedes the following noun it cannot be an adjective. Thirdly, Hebrew adjectives match the plurality or singularity of the noun it is describing. The following noun is plural and this word is singular. If this word was an adjective, it would also be in the plural.

יָמִים

Transliteration: yah-mim

Translation: days

Morphology: The base word is the masculine noun יוֹם (yom, Strong's #3117) meaning "day." The suffix יִם (iym) identifies the noun as plural.

Comments: When two nouns are placed together, such as with שֵׁשֶׁת and יָמִים, they are in the construct state and the word "of" would be placed between them in English—"six of the days."

עָשָׂה

Transliteration: a-sah

Translation: he made

Morphology: The word עשה (Ah-S-H, Strong's #6213) is a verb meaning "do." The lack of prefixes or suffixes to this verb identifies the tense of the verb as perfect tense, and the subject of the verb as third person, masculine singular - he did.

Comments: This verb is used in a wide variety of applications and is frequently used for "making."

יְהֹוָה

Transliteration: YHVH

Translation: YHVH

Morphology: The word יהוה (YHVH, Strong's #3068) is a name derived from the verb הוה (H-Y-H, Strong's #1961) with the prefix י (y) identifying the subject of this verb as third person, masculine singular. Therefore this name means "he exists."

Comments: The vowel pointings attached to this word were never meant for the pronunciation of this name. Instead, they are the vowel pointings from the word אדוני (adonai, Strong's #136), which is the word Jews speak when they see the name יהוה. The original pronunciation of this name is uncertain. YHVH is the subject of the previous verb, the "he" in "he made."

אֵת

Transliteration: et

Translation: [no translation for אֵת]

Morphology: The word אֵת (eyt, Strong's #853) is a particle that precedes the definite direct object of the previous verb.

הַשָּׁמַיִם

Transliteration: ha-sha-ma-yim

Translation: the sky

Morphology: The base word is the masculine noun שמים (shamayim, Strong's #8064) meaning "sky." The prefix ה (ha) is the article meaning "the."

Comments: This noun is the definite direct object of the previous verb.

וְאֵת

Transliteration: ve-et

Translation: and [no translation for אֵת]

Morphology: The word אֵת (eyt, Strong's #853) is a particle that precedes the definite direct object of the previous verb. The prefix ו (ve) is the conjunction meaning "and."

הָאָרֶץ

Transliteration: ha-a-rets

Translation: the land

Morphology: The base word is the masculine noun אֶרֶץ (erets, Strong's #776) meaning "land," or "region." The prefix ה (ha) is the article meaning "the."

Comments: This is also the definite direct object of the previous verb.

אֵת

Transliteration: et

Translation: [no translation for אֵת]

Morphology: The word אֵת (eyt, Strong's #853) is a particle that precedes the definite direct object of the previous verb.

הַיָּם

Transliteration: hai-yam

Translation: the sea

Morphology: The base word is the masculine noun יַם (yam, Strong's #3220) meaning "sea." The prefix ה (ha) is the article meaning "the."

Comments: Another definite direct object of the previous verb.

וְאֵת

Transliteration: ve-et

Translation: and [no translation for אֵת]

Morphology: The word אֵת (eyt, Strong's #853) is a particle that precedes the definite direct object of the previous verb. The prefix (ve) is the conjunction meaning "and."

כָּל

Transliteration: kol

Translation: all

Morphology: The word כל (kol, Strong's #3605) is a noun meaning "all."

אֲשֶׁר

Transliteration: ah-sher

Translation: that

Morphology: The word אשר (asher, Strong's #834) is the relative participle that can mean "which," "that," "what" or "who."

בָּם

Transliteration: bam

Translation: in them

Morphology: This word does not contain any base word, but includes the prefix בַּ (ba), a preposition meaning "in," and the third person, masculine plural pronoun suffix ם (m) meaning "them."

Comments: The phrase "all which are in them" is also a definite direct object of the previous verb.

וַיָּנַח

Transliteration: vai-ya-nahh

Translation: and he rested

Morphology: The root is the verb נוח (N-U-Hh, Strong's #5117) meaning "rest." When the verb is conjugated the letter ו (vav) is dropped. The prefix י (ye) identifies the verb as imperfect tense—"will rest;" and the subject of the verb as third person masculine singular—"he will rest." The prefix ו (va) is a conjunction meaning "and," but also reverses the tense of the verb to the perfect tense—"and he rested."

Comments: The subject of the verb, the "he" in "he rested," is YHVH, who is identified previously in this verse.

בַּיּוֹם

Transliteration: bai-yom

Translation: in the day

Morphology: The base word is the masculine noun יוֹם (yom, Strong's #3117) meaning "day." The prefix בּ (ba) is a preposition meaning "in."

הַשְּׁבִיעִי

Transliteration: hash-viy-iy

Translation: the seventh

Morphology: The base word is the adjective שביעי (sheviyiy, Strong's #7637) meaning "seventh." The prefix ה (ha) is the article meaning "the."

Comments: This adjective is describing the previous word, so the phrase "in-the–day the-seventh" would be translated as "in the seventh day."

עַל

Transliteration: al

Translation: upon

Morphology: The word על (al, Strong's #5921) is a preposition meaning "upon."

כֵּן

Transliteration: keyn

Translation: So

Morphology: The word כֵן (keyn, Strong's #3651) is the adverb meaning "so."

Comments: When this and the previous word are put together they mean "therefore."

בֵּרַךְ

Transliteration: bey-rakh

Translation: he showed respect

Morphology: The word ברך (B-R-K, Strong's #1288) is a verb meaning "kneel," but it is written in the piel form and means "to kneel before another to show respect." The lack of prefixes or suffixes to the verb identifies the tense of the verb as perfect tense, and the subject of the verb as third person, masculine singular - he showed respect.

יְהוָה

Transliteration: YHVH

Translation: YHVH

Morphology: The word יהוה (YHVH, Strong's #3068) is a name derived from the verb הוה (H-Y-H, Strong's #1961) with the prefix י (y) identifying the subject of this verb as third person, masculine singular. Therefore this name means "he exists."

Comments: This name is the subject of the previous verb, the "he" in "he showed respect."

The vowel pointings attached to this word were never meant for the pronunciation of this name. Instead, they are the vowel pointings from the word אֲדוֹנָי (adonai, Strong's #136), which is the word Jews speak when they see the name יהוה. The original pronunciation of this name is uncertain.

אֶת

Transliteration: et

Translation: [no translation for אֶת]

Morphology: The word אֶת (eyt, Strong's #853) is a particle that precedes the definite direct object of the previous verb.

יוֹם

Transliteration: yom

Translation: day

Morphology: The word יוֹם (yom, Strong's #3117) is a masculine noun meaning "day."

הַשַּׁבָּת

Transliteration: ha-shab-bat

Translation: the ceasing

Morphology: The base word is the noun שבת (Shabbat, Strong's #7676) meaning "ceasing." The prefix ה (ha) is the article meaning "the."

Comments: When two nouns are placed together, such as with יום and השבת, they are in the construct state and the word "of" would be placed between them in the English—"the day of ceasing" (note that the article shifts to the first noun in the phrase).

This phrase is the definite direct object of the previous verb.

וַיְקַדְּשֵׁהוּ

Transliteration: vai-qad-shey-hu

Translation: and he set him apart as special

Morphology: The root is the verb קדש (Q-D-Sh, Strong's #6942) meaning "set apart for a special purpose." The prefix י (ye) identifies the verb as imperfect tense—"will set apart;" and the subject of the verb as third person masculine singular—"he will set apart." The prefix ו (va) is a conjunction meaning "and," but also reverses the tense of the verb to the perfect tense—"and he set apart." The suffix הו (hu) identifies the object of the verb as third person, masculine singular—"and he set him apart."

Comments: The subject of the verb, the "he" in "he showed respect," is YHVH, who is identified previously in this verse. The object of the verb, the "him," is referring to the "day," a masculine word in Hebrew.

A Literal Translation

Because six of the days YHVH made the sky
and the land, the sea and all that are in
them, and he rested in the seventh day,
therefore YHVH showed respect to the day
of ceasing and he set him apart as special.

Exodus 20:12

כַּבֵּד אֶת־אָבִיךָ וְאֶת־אִמֶּךָ לְמַעַן
יַאֲרִכוּן יָמֶיךָ עַל הָאֲדָמָה אֲשֶׁר־יְהֹוָה
אֱלֹהֶיךָ נֹתֵן לָךְ :

כַּבֵּד

Transliteration: ka-beyd

Translation: honor

Morphology: The word כבד (K-B-D, Strong's #3513) is a verb meaning "be heavy," but is written in the piel imperative form and means "honor" in the sense of giving weight to another.

אֶת

Transliteration: et

Translation: [no translation for את]

Morphology: The word את (eyt, Strong's #853) is a particle that precedes the definite direct object of the previous verb.

אָבִיךָ

Transliteration: a-viy-kha

Translation: your father

Morphology: The base word is the masculine noun אב (av, Strong's #1) meaning "father." The suffix י (iy) identifies the verb as a construct (This suffix is rare in Biblical Hebrew). The suffix ךָ (kha) is the second person, masculine singular, possessive pronoun—"of you" or "your."

Comments: This noun is the definite direct object of the previous verb.

וְאֵת

Transliteration: ve-et

Translation: and [no translation for אֵת]

Morphology: The word אֵת (eyt, Strong's #853) is a particle that precedes the definite direct object of the previous verb. The prefix ו (ve) is the conjunction meaning "and."

אִמֶּךָ

Transliteration: i-meh-kha

Translation: your mother

Morphology: The base word is the feminine noun אֵם (eym, Strong's #517) meaning "mother." The suffix ךָ

(kha) is the second person, masculine singular, possessive pronoun—"of you" or "your."

Comments: This noun is also a definite direct object of the previous verb.

לְמַעַן

Transliteration: le-ma-an

Translation: in order that

Morphology: The word למען (le'ma'an, Strong's #4616) is a preposition meaning "in order that."

יַאֲרִכוּן

Transliteration: ya-a-riy-khun

Translation: they will certainly be long

Morphology: The root is the verb ארך (A-R-K, Strong's #748) meaning "be long." The prefix י (ya) and the suffix ו (u) identify the verb as imperfect tense, and the subject of the verb as third person, masculine plural—"they will be long." The suffix ן (n) is called the paragogic nun, which adds the idea of "must" or "certainly" to the verb— "they will certainly be long."

יָמֶיךָ

Transliteration: ya-mey-kha

Translation: your days

Morphology: The base word is the masculine noun יוֹם (yom, Strong's #3117) meaning "day." The suffix יַ (iym) identifies the noun as plural, but in the construct state the letter ם (m) is dropped. The suffix ך (kha) is the second person, masculine singular, possessive pronoun—"of you" or "your."

Comments: This word is the object of the previous verb, the "they," in "they will certainly be long."

עַל

Transliteration: al

Translation: upon

Morphology: The word עַל (al, Strong's #5921) is a preposition meaning "upon."

הָאֲדָמָה

Transliteration: ha-a-da-mah

Translation: the ground

Morphology: The base word is the feminine noun אדמה (adamah, Strong's #127) meaning "ground." The prefix ה (ha) is the article meaning "the."

אֲשֶׁר

Transliteration: ah-sher

Translation: which

Morphology: The word אשר (asher, Strong's #834) is the relative participle that can mean "which," "that," "what" or "who."

יְהוָה

Transliteration: YHVH

Translation: YHVH

Morphology: The word יהוה (YHVH, Strong's #3068) is a name derived from the verb הוה (H-Y-H, Strong's #1961) with the prefix י (y) identifying the subject of this verb as third person, masculine singular. Therefore this name means "he exists."

Comments: The vowel pointings attached to this word were never meant for the pronunciation of this name. Instead, they are the vowel pointings from the word אדוני (adonai, Strong's #136), which is the word Jews speak when they see the name יהוה. The original pronunciation of this name is uncertain.

אֱלֹהֶיךָ

Transliteration: eh-lo-hey-kha

Translation: your powerful one

Morphology: The base word is the noun אלוה (elo'ah, Strong's #433) meaning "power" or "powerful one." The י (iym) is the masculine plural suffix, but in the construct state the letter ם (m) is dropped. The suffix ך (kha) is the second person, masculine singular, possessive pronoun—"of you" or "your."

Comments: This plural noun is often used for someone or something of great importance or stature and the context of its use will determine if this word is being used as singular or plural.

Because this word is describing YHVH, a singular, this noun is being used as a singular.

נֹתֵן

Transliteration: no-teyn

Translation: giving

Morphology: The word נתן (N-T-N, Strong's #5414) is a verb meaning "give," but is written in the participle form (identified by the "o" and "ey" vowel pointings)—"giving."

לָךְ

Transliteration: lakh

Translation: to you

Morphology: This word does not contain any base word, but includes the prefix ל (la), a preposition meaning "to," and the second person, masculine singular pronoun suffix ך (kh) meaning "you."

A Literal Translation

Give honor to your father and your mother in order that your days will certainly be long upon the ground, which YHVH your powerful one is giving to you.

Exodus 20:13

לֹא תִּרְצָח׃

לֹא

Transliteration: lo

Translation: not

Morphology: The word לֹא (lo, Strong's #3808) is the negative participle meaning "not" and negates the action of the next verb.

תִּרְצָח

Transliteration: tir-tsahh

Translation: you will murder

Morphology: The root is the verb רצח (R-Ts-Hh, Strong's #7523) meaning "murder." The prefix ת (ti) identifies the verb as imperfect tense—"will murder;" and the subject of the verb as second person masculine singular—"you will murder."

Comments: Because of the negative participle preceding this verb, the verb will be translated as "you will not murder."

A Literal Translation

You will not murder.

Exodus 20:14

לֹא תִנְאָף׃

לֹא

Transliteration: lo

Translation: not

Morphology: The word לֹא (lo, Strong's #3808) is the negative participle meaning "not" and negates the action of the next verb.

תִנְאָף

Transliteration: tin-aph

Translation: you will commit adultery

Morphology: The root is the verb נאף (N-A-Ph, Strong's #5003) meaning "commit adultery." The prefix ת (ti) identifies the verb as imperfect tense—"will commit adultery;" and the subject of the verb as second person masculine singular—"you will commit adultery."

Comments: Because of the negative participle preceding this verb, the verb will be translated as "you will not commit adultery."

A Literal Translation

You will not commit adultery.

Exodus 20:15

לֹא תִגְנֹב:

לֹא

Transliteration: lo

Translation: not

Morphology: The word לֹא (lo, Strong's #3808) is the negative participle meaning "not" and negates the action of the next verb.

תִגְנֹב

Transliteration: tig-nov

Translation: you will steal

Morphology: The root is the verb גנב (G-N-B, Strong's #1589) meaning "steal." The prefix ת (ti) identifies the verb as imperfect tense—"will steal;" and the subject of the verb as second person masculine singular—"you will steal."

Comments: Because of the negative participle preceding this verb, the verb will be translated as "you will not steal."

A Literal Translation

You will not steal.

Exodus 20:16

לֹא־תַעֲנֶה בְרֵעֲךָ עֵד שָׁקֶר׃

לֹא

Transliteration: lo

Translation: not

Morphology: The word לֹא (lo, Strong's #3808) is the negative participle meaning "not" and negates the action of the next verb.

תַעֲנֶה

Transliteration: tah-ah-neh

Translation: you will answer

Morphology: The root is the verb ענה (A-N-H, Strong's #6030) meaning "answer." The prefix ת (ta) identifies the verb as imperfect tense—"will answer;" and the subject of the verb as second person masculine singular—"you will answer."

Comments: Because of the negative participle preceding this verb, the verb will be translated as "you will not answer."

בְּרֵעֶךָ

Transliteration: be-rey-ah-kha

Translation: with your friend

Morphology: The base word is the masculine noun רֵע (ra, Strong's #7453) meaning "friend" or "companion." The prefix בּ (be) is a preposition meaning "in" or "with." The suffix ךָ (kha) is the second person, masculine singular, possessive pronoun—"of you" or "your."

עֵד

Transliteration: eyd

Translation: witness

Morphology: The word עֵד (eyd, Strong's #5707) is a noun meaning "witness."

שָׁקֶר

Transliteration: shah-qehr

Translation: deception

Morphology: The word שקר (sheqer, Strong's #8267) is a noun meaning "deception."

Comments: When two nouns are placed together, such as with עֵד and שקר, they are in the construct state and the word "of" would be placed between them in the English—"witness of deception."

A Literal Translation

You will not answer a witness of deception with your friend.

Exodus 20:17

לֹא תַחְמֹד בֵּית רֵעֶךָ לֹא־תַחְמֹד אֵשֶׁת
רֵעֶךָ וְעַבְדּוֹ וַאֲמָתוֹ וְשׁוֹרוֹ וַחֲמֹרוֹ וְכֹל
אֲשֶׁר לְרֵעֶךָ׃

לֹא

Transliteration: lo

Translation: not

Morphology: The word לֹא (lo, Strong's #3808) is the negative participle meaning "not" and negates the action of the next verb.

תַחְמֹד

Transliteration: tahh-mod

Translation: you will desire

Morphology: The root is the verb חמד (Hh-M-D, Strong's #2530) meaning "desire." The prefix ת (ta) identifies the verb as imperfect tense–"will desire;" and the subject of the verb as second person masculine singular–"you will desire."

Comments: Because of the negative participle preceding this verb, the verb will be translated as "you will not desire."

בַּיִת

Transliteration: beyt

Translation: house

Morphology: The base word is the masculine noun בית (bayit, Strong's #1004) meaning "house."

רֵעֶךָ

Transliteration: rey-eh-kha

Translation: your friend

Morphology: The base word is the masculine noun רע (ra, Strong's #7453) meaning "friend" or "companion." The suffix ך (kha) is the second person, masculine singular, possessive pronoun—"of you" or "your."

Comments: When two nouns are placed together, such as with בית and רעך, they are in the construct state and the word "of" would be placed between them in the English—"house of your friend."

לֹא

Transliteration: lo

Translation: not

Morphology: The word לֹא (lo, Strong's #3808) is the negative participle meaning "not" and negates the action of the next verb.

תַחְמֹד

Transliteration: tahh-mod

Translation: you will desire

Morphology: The root is the verb חמד (Hh-M-D, Strong's #2530) meaning "desire." The prefix ת (ta) identifies the verb as imperfect tense—"will desire;" and the subject of the verb as second person masculine singular—"you will desire."

Comments: Because of the negative participle preceding this verb, the verb will be translated as "you will not desire."

אֵשֶׁת

Transliteration: ey-shet

Translation: woman

Morphology: The base word is the feminine noun אשה (iyshah, Strong's #802) meaning "woman."

Comments: When a feminine noun ends with the letter ה (hey) and is in construct state, the ה is converted to a ת (tav). When the noun "woman" is used in the possessive it means "wife."

רֵעֶךָ

Transliteration: rey-eh-kha

Translation: your friend

Morphology: The base word is the masculine noun רע (ra, Strong's #7453) meaning "friend" or "companion." The suffix ךָ (kha) is the second person, masculine singular, possessive pronoun—"of you" or "your."

Comments: When two nouns are placed together, such as with אשת and רעך, they are in the construct state and the word "of" would be placed between them in the English—"woman of your friend."

וְעַבְדּוֹ

Transliteration: ve-av-do

Translation: or his slave

Morphology: The base word is the masculine noun עבד (eved, Strong's #5650) meaning "slave." The prefix ו (ve) is a conjunction meaning "and," but in context this is better translated as "or" in this verse. The suffix ו (o) is the third person, masculine singular, and possessive pronoun "of him" or "his."

וַאֲמָתוֹ

Transliteration: va-a-ma-to

Translation: or his maid-servant

Morphology: The base word is the feminine noun אמה (amah, Strong's #519) meaning "maid-servant." The prefix ו (va) is the conjunction meaning "and," but in context this is better translated as "or" in this verse. The suffix ו (kha) is the third person, masculine singular, possessive pronoun—"of him" or "his."

Comments: When a feminine noun ends with the letter ה (hey) and is in construct state, the ה is converted to a ת (tav).

וְשׁוֹרוֹ

Transliteration: ve-shor-o

Translation: or his ox

Morphology: The base word is the feminine noun שׁוֹר (shor, Strong's #7794) meaning "ox." The prefix ו (ve) is the conjunction meaning "and," but in context this is better translated as "or" in this verse. The suffix ו (kha) is the third person, masculine singular, possessive pronoun—"of him" or "his."

וַחֲמֹרוֹ

Transliteration: va-hha-mo-ro

Translation: or his donkey

Morphology: The base word is the feminine noun חֲמוֹר (hhamor, Strong's #2543) meaning "Donkey." The prefix ו (va) is the conjunction meaning "and," but in context this is better translated as "or" in this verse. The suffix וֹ (kha) is the third person, masculine singular, possessive pronoun–"of him" or "his."

וְכָל

Transliteration: ve-khol

Translation: or anything

Morphology: The base word is the noun כל (kol, Strong's #3605) meaning "all" or "anything." The prefix ו (ve) is a conjunction meaning "and," but in context this is better translated as "or" in this verse.

אֲשֶׁר

Transliteration: ah-sher

Translation: that

Morphology: The word אשר (asher, Strong's #834) is the relative participle that can mean "which," "that," "what" or "who."

לְרֵעֶךָ

Transliteration: le-rey-eh-kha

Translation: belongs to your friend

Morphology: The base word is the masculine noun רע (ra, Strong's #7453) meaning "friend" or "companion."

The prefix ל (le) is a preposition meaning "to" or "belongs to." The suffix ך (kha) is the second person, masculine singular, possessive pronoun—"of you" or "your."

A Literal Translation

You will not desire the house of your friend; you will not desire the woman of your friend, or his slave, or his maid-servant, or his ox, or his donkey, or anything that belongs to your friend.